What Momma says about... Grief

by
Charlene Helm

Illustrated by
Ealasaid L. Witt

HELM GROUP
Vancouver, Canada

ISBN: 1543018394
ISBN-13: 978-1543018394

acknowledgements

From the author:

This special edition is dedicated to my late father, Raymond Helm, who inspired me to write about this topic. He taught me life's most precious lesson which is to live with passion, purpose and love.

I also want to offer a heart felt thank you to my loving daughter Solayah and all of our friends and family who have supported us through some of life's most torrential storms. Thank you for holding us close.

From the illustrator:

This is for my own late father, Charles Beard Sanford. His lessons and legacy are many, but, through his presence, I learned to appreciate each day and never take the time we have with others for granted.
Love and miss you, Dad.

Momma says...

I have feelings as deep, **blue** and as **wide** as the sea.

Sometimes they're **rough** and choppy, or *smooth* and **calm** as can be.

Momma says...

that some feelings are **heavy**
and other ones feel light,

Some feelings help me
go to sleep while others
keep me up all night.

Momma says...

tears wash away sadness
when they glimmer
down my cheek,

8

It feels like I'm filling puddles
because I've cried so much
this week.

Momma says...

it's okay to feel
glum and blue...

She wants to
make sure I'm okay
so talking is
good to do.

Momma says...

Writing down my worries or **coloring** about how I feel...

Scribbling out my angry thoughts...
these things help me heal.

Momma says...

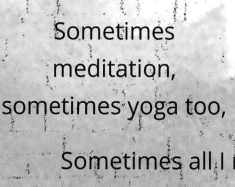

Sometimes
meditation,
sometimes yoga too,

Sometimes all I need
are friends or
something fun to do.

Momma says...

"Remember, they
are still with
you everyday.

Sometimes...
...people say goodbye
but their spirit
always stays.

Momma says...

Remember that they love you
and watch you from afar.

Remember them before
you sleep and blow a kiss
towards the stars.

Momma says...

Remember them in happy times
and for all the fun times
that you had,

Celebrate how much they
loved you and how that
makes you glad.

Momma says...

My love, please do not worry,
because I'm here to
hold you tight,

So let's snuggle up
with baby bear,
and in time,
you'll feel all right.

For our Dads.

92874464R00015

Made in the USA
Columbia, SC
05 April 2018